Hiking Journal

Belongs to:

_____

Location: _____

Date: _____ Weather: _____ Temperature: _____

Start time: _____ End time: _____ Total distance: _____

Hike rating: ☆ ☆ ☆ ☆ ☆ Difficulty: 1 2 3 4 5

Trail type: _____ Elevation gain/loss: _____

Trail(s): _____

_____

Terrain: _____

_____

Companions: _____

_____

_____

Facilities / Water availability?: _____

_____

_____

Observations (nature, wildlife, other): _____

_____

_____

Favorite moment: _____

_____

_____

To do next time: _____

_____

_____

NOTES:

_____

_____

_____

_____

_____

_____

_____

_____

_____

PHOTO/DRAWING:

Location: _____

Date: _____ Weather: _____ Temperature: _____

Start time: _____ End time: _____ Total distance: _____

Hike rating: ☆ ☆ ☆ ☆ ☆   Difficulty: 1 2 3 4 5

Trail type: _____ Elevation gain/loss: _____

Trail(s): _____

_____

Terrain: _____

_____

Companions: _____

_____

_____

Facilities / Water availability?: _____

_____

_____

Observations (nature, wildlife, other): _____

_____

_____

Favorite moment: _____

_____

_____

To do next time: _____

_____

_____

NOTES:

_____

_____

_____

_____

_____

_____

_____

_____

_____

_____

_____

PHOTO/DRAWING:

Location: _____

Date: _____ Weather: _____ Temperature: _____

Start time: _____ End time: _____ Total distance: _____

Hike rating: ☆ ☆ ☆ ☆ ☆   Difficulty: 1 2 3 4 5

Trail type: _____ Elevation gain/loss: _____

Trail(s): _____
_____

Terrain: _____
_____

Companions: _____
_____
_____

Facilities / Water availability?: _____
_____
_____

Observations (nature, wildlife, other): _____
_____
_____

Favorite moment: _____
_____
_____

To do next time: _____
_____
_____

NOTES:

_____

_____

_____

_____

_____

_____

_____

_____

_____

_____

_____

PHOTO/DRAWING:

Location: _____

Date: _____ Weather: _____ Temperature: _____

Start time: _____ End time: _____ Total distance: _____

Hike rating: ☆ ☆ ☆ ☆ ☆   Difficulty: 1 2 3 4 5

Trail type: _____ Elevation gain/loss: _____

Trail(s): _____

_____

Terrain: _____

_____

Companions: _____

_____

_____

Facilities / Water availability?: _____

_____

_____

Observations (nature, wildlife, other): _____

_____

_____

Favorite moment: _____

_____

_____

To do next time: _____

_____

_____

NOTES:

_____

_____

_____

_____

_____

_____

_____

_____

_____

_____

PHOTO/DRAWING:

Location: _____

Date: _____ Weather: _____ Temperature: _____

Start time: _____ End time: _____ Total distance: _____

Hike rating: ☆ ☆ ☆ ☆ ☆   Difficulty: 1 2 3 4 5

Trail type: _____ Elevation gain/loss: _____

Trail(s): _____

_____

Terrain: _____

_____

Companions: _____

_____

_____

Facilities / Water availability?: _____

_____

_____

Observations (nature, wildlife, other): _____

_____

_____

Favorite moment: _____

_____

_____

To do next time: _____

_____

_____

NOTES:

_____

_____

_____

_____

_____

_____

_____

_____

_____

_____

_____

PHOTO/DRAWING:

Location: _____

Date: _____ Weather: _____ Temperature: _____

Start time: _____ End time: _____ Total distance: _____

Hike rating: ☆ ☆ ☆ ☆ ☆   Difficulty: 1 2 3 4 5

Trail type: _____ Elevation gain/loss: _____

Trail(s): _____

_____

Terrain: _____

_____

Companions: _____

_____

_____

Facilities / Water availability?: _____

_____

_____

Observations (nature, wildlife, other): _____

_____

_____

Favorite moment: _____

_____

_____

To do next time: _____

_____

_____

NOTES:

_____

_____

_____

_____

_____

_____

_____

_____

_____

_____

_____

PHOTO/DRAWING:

Location: _____

Date: _____ Weather: _____ Temperature: _____

Start time: _____ End time: _____ Total distance: _____

Hike rating: ☆ ☆ ☆ ☆ ☆   Difficulty: 1 2 3 4 5

Trail type: _____ Elevation gain/loss: _____

Trail(s): _____

_____

Terrain: _____

_____

Companions: _____

_____

_____

Facilities / Water availability?: _____

_____

_____

Observations (nature, wildlife, other): _____

_____

_____

Favorite moment: _____

_____

_____

To do next time: _____

_____

_____

NOTES:

_____

_____

_____

_____

_____

_____

_____

_____

_____

_____

PHOTO/DRAWING:

Location: _____

Date: _____ Weather: _____ Temperature: _____

Start time: _____ End time: _____ Total distance: _____

Hike rating: ☆ ☆ ☆ ☆ ☆ Difficulty: 1 2 3 4 5

Trail type: _____ Elevation gain/loss: _____

Trail(s): _____

_____

Terrain: _____

_____

Companions: _____

_____

_____

Facilities / Water availability?: _____

_____

_____

Observations (nature, wildlife, other): _____

_____

_____

Favorite moment: _____

_____

_____

To do next time: _____

_____

_____

NOTES:

PHOTO/DRAWING:

Location: _____

Date: _____ Weather: _____ Temperature: _____

Start time: _____ End time: _____ Total distance: _____

Hike rating: ☆ ☆ ☆ ☆ ☆   Difficulty: 1 2 3 4 5

Trail type: _____ Elevation gain/loss: _____

Trail(s): _____

_____

Terrain: _____

_____

Companions: _____

_____

_____

Facilities / Water availability?: _____

_____

_____

Observations (nature, wildlife, other): _____

_____

_____

Favorite moment: _____

_____

_____

To do next time: _____

_____

_____

NOTES: _____

_____

_____

_____

_____

_____

_____

_____

_____

_____

PHOTO/DRAWING:

LOCATION: _____

DATE: _____ WEATHER: _____ TEMPERATURE: _____

START TIME: _____ END TIME: _____ TOTAL DISTANCE: _____

HIKE RATING: ☆ ☆ ☆ ☆ ☆   DIFFICULTY: 1 2 3 4 5

TRAIL TYPE: _____ ELEVATION GAIN/LOSS: _____

TRAIL(S): _____

_____

TERRAIN: _____

_____

COMPANIONS: _____

_____

_____

FACILITIES / WATER AVAILABILITY?: _____

_____

_____

OBSERVATIONS (NATURE, WILDLIFE, OTHER): _____

_____

_____

FAVORITE MOMENT: _____

_____

_____

TO DO NEXT TIME: _____

_____

_____

NOTES:

_____

_____

_____

_____

_____

_____

_____

_____

_____

_____

_____

PHOTO/DRAWING:

Location: _____

Date: _____ Weather: _____ Temperature: _____

Start time: _____ End time: _____ Total distance: _____

Hike rating: ☆ ☆ ☆ ☆ ☆   Difficulty: 1 2 3 4 5

Trail type: _____ Elevation gain/loss: _____

Trail(s): _____

_____

Terrain: _____

_____

Companions: _____

_____

_____

Facilities / Water availability?: _____

_____

_____

Observations (nature, wildlife, other): _____

_____

_____

Favorite moment: _____

_____

_____

To do next time: _____

_____

_____

NOTES:

_____

_____

_____

_____

_____

_____

_____

_____

_____

_____

PHOTO/DRAWING:

Location: _____

Date: _____ Weather: _____ Temperature: _____

Start time: _____ End time: _____ Total distance: _____

Hike rating: ☆ ☆ ☆ ☆ ☆   Difficulty: 1 2 3 4 5

Trail type: _____ Elevation gain/loss: _____

Trail(s): _____

_____

Terrain: _____

_____

Companions: _____

_____

_____

Facilities / Water availability?: _____

_____

_____

Observations (nature, wildlife, other): _____

_____

_____

Favorite moment: _____

_____

_____

To do next time: _____

_____

_____

NOTES:

_____

_____

_____

_____

_____

_____

_____

_____

_____

_____

_____

PHOTO/DRAWING:

Location: _____

Date: _____ Weather: _____ Temperature: _____

Start time: _____ End time: _____ Total distance: _____

Hike rating: ☆ ☆ ☆ ☆ ☆   Difficulty: 1 2 3 4 5

Trail type: _____ Elevation gain/loss: _____

Trail(s): _____

_____

Terrain: _____

_____

Companions: _____

_____

_____

Facilities / Water availability?: _____

_____

_____

Observations (nature, wildlife, other): _____

_____

_____

Favorite moment: _____

_____

_____

To do next time: _____

_____

_____

NOTES:

_____

_____

_____

_____

_____

_____

_____

_____

_____

_____

PHOTO/DRAWING:

Location: _____

Date: _____ Weather: _____ Temperature: _____

Start time: _____ End time: _____ Total distance: _____

Hike rating: ☆ ☆ ☆ ☆ ☆ Difficulty: 1 2 3 4 5

Trail type: _____ Elevation gain/loss: _____

Trail(s): _____

_____

Terrain: _____

_____

Companions: _____

_____

_____

Facilities / Water availability?: _____

_____

_____

Observations (nature, wildlife, other): _____

_____

_____

Favorite moment: _____

_____

_____

To do next time: _____

_____

_____

NOTES:

_____

_____

_____

_____

_____

_____

_____

_____

_____

PHOTO/DRAWING:

Location: _____

Date: _____ Weather: _____ Temperature: _____

Start time: _____ End time: _____ Total distance: _____

Hike rating: ☆ ☆ ☆ ☆ ☆ Difficulty: 1 2 3 4 5

Trail type: _____ Elevation gain/loss: _____

Trail(s): _____

_____

Terrain: _____

_____

Companions: _____

_____

_____

Facilities / Water availability?: _____

_____

_____

Observations (nature, wildlife, other): _____

_____

_____

Favorite moment: _____

_____

_____

To do next time: _____

_____

_____

NOTES:

_____

_____

_____

_____

_____

_____

_____

_____

_____

_____

PHOTO/DRAWING:

Location: _____

Date: _____ Weather: _____ Temperature: _____

Start time: _____ End time: _____ Total distance: _____

Hike rating: ☆ ☆ ☆ ☆ ☆   Difficulty: 1 2 3 4 5

Trail type: _____ Elevation gain/loss: _____

Trail(s): _____
_____

Terrain: _____
_____

Companions: _____
_____
_____

Facilities / Water availability?: _____
_____
_____

Observations (nature, wildlife, other): _____
_____
_____

Favorite moment: _____
_____
_____

To do next time: _____
_____
_____

NOTES: _____

_____

_____

_____

_____

_____

_____

_____

_____

_____

_____

PHOTO/DRAWING:

Location: _____

Date: _____ Weather: _____ Temperature: _____

Start time: _____ End time: _____ Total distance: _____

Hike rating: ☆ ☆ ☆ ☆ ☆ Difficulty: 1 2 3 4 5

Trail type: _____ Elevation gain/loss: _____

Trail(s): _____

_____

Terrain: _____

_____

Companions: _____

_____

_____

Facilities / Water availability?: _____

_____

_____

Observations (nature, wildlife, other): _____

_____

_____

Favorite moment: _____

_____

_____

To do next time: _____

_____

_____

NOTES:

_____

_____

_____

_____

_____

_____

_____

_____

_____

_____

_____

PHOTO/DRAWING:

Location: _____

Date: _____ Weather: _____ Temperature: _____

Start time: _____ End time: _____ Total distance: _____

Hike rating: ☆ ☆ ☆ ☆ ☆   Difficulty: 1 2 3 4 5

Trail type: _____ Elevation gain/loss: _____

Trail(s): _____

_____

Terrain: _____

_____

Companions: _____

_____

_____

Facilities / Water availability?: _____

_____

_____

Observations (nature, wildlife, other): _____

_____

_____

Favorite moment: _____

_____

_____

To do next time: _____

_____

_____

NOTES:

_____

_____

_____

_____

_____

_____

_____

_____

_____

_____

_____

PHOTO/DRAWING:

Location: _____

Date: _____ Weather: _____ Temperature: _____

Start time: _____ End time: _____ Total distance: _____

Hike rating: ☆ ☆ ☆ ☆ ☆   Difficulty: 1 2 3 4 5

Trail type: _____ Elevation gain/loss: _____

Trail(s): _____

_____

Terrain: _____

_____

Companions: _____

_____

_____

Facilities / Water availability?: _____

_____

_____

Observations (nature, wildlife, other): _____

_____

_____

Favorite moment: _____

_____

_____

To do next time: _____

_____

_____

NOTES:

_____

_____

_____

_____

_____

_____

_____

_____

_____

_____

PHOTO/DRAWING:

Location: _____

Date: _____ Weather: _____ Temperature: _____

Start time: _____ End time: _____ Total distance: _____

Hike rating: ☆ ☆ ☆ ☆ ☆   Difficulty: 1 2 3 4 5

Trail type: _____ Elevation gain/loss: _____

Trail(s): _____

_____

Terrain: _____

_____

Companions: _____

_____

_____

Facilities / Water availability?: _____

_____

_____

Observations (nature, wildlife, other): _____

_____

_____

Favorite moment: _____

_____

_____

To do next time: _____

_____

_____

NOTES: _____

_____

_____

_____

_____

_____

_____

_____

_____

_____

PHOTO/DRAWING:

Location: _____

Date: _____ Weather: _____ Temperature: _____

Start time: _____ End time: _____ Total distance: _____

Hike rating: ☆ ☆ ☆ ☆ ☆   Difficulty: 1 2 3 4 5

Trail type: _____ Elevation gain/loss: _____

Trail(s): _____

_____

Terrain: _____

_____

Companions: _____

_____

_____

Facilities / Water availability?: _____

_____

_____

Observations (nature, wildlife, other): _____

_____

_____

Favorite moment: _____

_____

_____

To do next time: _____

_____

_____

NOTES:

_____

_____

_____

_____

_____

_____

_____

_____

_____

_____

PHOTO/DRAWING:

Location: _____

Date: _____ Weather: _____ Temperature: _____

Start time: _____ End time: _____ Total distance: _____

Hike rating: ☆ ☆ ☆ ☆ ☆   Difficulty: 1 2 3 4 5

Trail type: _____ Elevation gain/loss: _____

Trail(s): _____

_____

Terrain: _____

_____

Companions: _____

_____

_____

Facilities / Water availability?: _____

_____

_____

Observations (nature, wildlife, other): _____

_____

_____

Favorite moment: _____

_____

_____

To do next time: _____

_____

_____

NOTES:

_____

_____

_____

_____

_____

_____

_____

_____

_____

PHOTO/DRAWING:

Location: _____

Date: _____ Weather: _____ Temperature: _____

Start time: _____ End time: _____ Total distance: _____

Hike rating: ☆ ☆ ☆ ☆ ☆   Difficulty: 1 2 3 4 5

Trail type: _____ Elevation gain/loss: _____

Trail(s): _____
_____

Terrain: _____
_____

Companions: _____
_____
_____

Facilities / Water availability?: _____
_____
_____

Observations (nature, wildlife, other): _____
_____
_____

Favorite moment: _____
_____
_____

To do next time: _____
_____
_____

NOTES:

_____

_____

_____

_____

_____

_____

_____

_____

_____

_____

PHOTO/DRAWING:

Location: _____

Date: _____ Weather: _____ Temperature: _____

Start time: _____ End time: _____ Total distance: _____

Hike rating: ☆ ☆ ☆ ☆ ☆   Difficulty: 1 2 3 4 5

Trail type: _____ Elevation gain/loss: _____

Trail(s): _____

_____

Terrain: _____

_____

Companions: _____

_____

_____

Facilities / Water availability?: _____

_____

_____

Observations (nature, wildlife, other): _____

_____

_____

Favorite moment: _____

_____

_____

To do next time: _____

_____

_____

NOTES:

_____

_____

_____

_____

_____

_____

_____

_____

_____

_____

PHOTO/DRAWING:

Location: _____

Date: _____ Weather: _____ Temperature: _____

Start time: _____ End time: _____ Total distance: _____

Hike rating: ☆ ☆ ☆ ☆ ☆   Difficulty: 1 2 3 4 5

Trail type: _____ Elevation gain/loss: _____

Trail(s): _____

_____

Terrain: _____

_____

Companions: _____

_____

_____

Facilities / Water availability?: _____

_____

_____

Observations (nature, wildlife, other): _____

_____

_____

Favorite moment: _____

_____

_____

To do next time: _____

_____

_____

NOTES: _____

_____

_____

_____

_____

_____

_____

_____

_____

_____

PHOTO/DRAWING:

Location: _____

Date: _____ Weather: _____ Temperature: _____

Start time: _____ End time: _____ Total distance: _____

Hike rating: ☆ ☆ ☆ ☆ ☆   Difficulty: 1 2 3 4 5

Trail type: _____ Elevation gain/loss: _____

Trail(s): _____

_____

Terrain: _____

_____

Companions: _____

_____

_____

Facilities / Water availability?: _____

_____

_____

Observations (nature, wildlife, other): _____

_____

_____

Favorite moment: _____

_____

_____

To do next time: _____

_____

_____

NOTES: _____

_____

_____

_____

_____

_____

_____

_____

_____

_____

PHOTO/DRAWING:

Location: _____

Date: _____ Weather: _____ Temperature: _____

Start time: _____ End time: _____ Total distance: _____

Hike rating: ☆ ☆ ☆ ☆ ☆   Difficulty: 1 2 3 4 5

Trail type: _____ Elevation gain/loss: _____

Trail(s): _____

_____

Terrain: _____

_____

Companions: _____

_____

_____

Facilities / Water availability?: _____

_____

_____

Observations (nature, wildlife, other): _____

_____

_____

Favorite moment: _____

_____

_____

To do next time: _____

_____

_____

NOTES: _____

_____

_____

_____

_____

_____

_____

_____

_____

_____

_____

PHOTO/DRAWING:

Location: _____

Date: _____ Weather: _____ Temperature: _____

Start time: _____ End time: _____ Total distance: _____

Hike rating: ☆ ☆ ☆ ☆ ☆   Difficulty: 1 2 3 4 5

Trail type: _____ Elevation gain/loss: _____

Trail(s): _____

_____

Terrain: _____

_____

Companions: _____

_____

_____

Facilities / Water availability?: _____

_____

_____

Observations (nature, wildlife, other): _____

_____

_____

Favorite moment: _____

_____

_____

To do next time: _____

_____

_____

NOTES:

_____

_____

_____

_____

_____

_____

_____

_____

_____

_____

_____

PHOTO/DRAWING:

Location: _____

Date: _____ Weather: _____ Temperature: _____

Start time: _____ End time: _____ Total distance: _____

Hike rating: ☆ ☆ ☆ ☆ ☆   Difficulty: 1 2 3 4 5

Trail type: _____ Elevation gain/loss: _____

Trail(s): _____

_____

Terrain: _____

_____

Companions: _____

_____

_____

Facilities / Water availability?: _____

_____

_____

Observations (nature, wildlife, other): _____

_____

_____

Favorite moment: _____

_____

_____

To do next time: _____

_____

_____

NOTES:

_____

_____

_____

_____

_____

_____

_____

_____

_____

_____

_____

PHOTO/DRAWING:

Location: _____

Date: _____ Weather: _____ Temperature: _____

Start time: _____ End time: _____ Total distance: _____

Hike rating: ☆ ☆ ☆ ☆ ☆ Difficulty: 1 2 3 4 5

Trail type: _____ Elevation gain/loss: _____

Trail(s): _____

_____

Terrain: _____

_____

Companions: _____

_____

_____

Facilities / Water availability?: _____

_____

_____

Observations (nature, wildlife, other): _____

_____

_____

Favorite moment: _____

_____

_____

To do next time: _____

_____

_____

NOTES:

_____

_____

_____

_____

_____

_____

_____

_____

_____

_____

_____

PHOTO/DRAWING:

Location: _____

Date: _____ Weather: _____ Temperature: _____

Start time: _____ End time: _____ Total distance: _____

Hike rating: ☆ ☆ ☆ ☆ ☆ Difficulty: 1 2 3 4 5

Trail type: _____ Elevation gain/loss: _____

Trail(s): _____

_____

Terrain: _____

_____

Companions: _____

_____

_____

Facilities / Water availability?: _____

_____

_____

Observations (nature, wildlife, other): _____

_____

_____

Favorite moment: _____

_____

_____

To do next time: _____

_____

_____

NOTES:

_____

_____

_____

_____

_____

_____

_____

_____

_____

_____

PHOTO/DRAWING:

Location: _____

Date: _____ Weather: _____ Temperature: _____

Start time: _____ End time: _____ Total distance: _____

Hike rating: ☆ ☆ ☆ ☆ ☆ Difficulty: 1 2 3 4 5

Trail type: _____ Elevation gain/loss: _____

Trail(s): _____

_____

Terrain: _____

_____

Companions: _____

_____

_____

Facilities / Water availability?: _____

_____

_____

Observations (nature, wildlife, other): _____

_____

_____

Favorite moment: _____

_____

_____

To do next time: _____

_____

_____

NOTES: _____

_____

_____

_____

_____

_____

_____

_____

_____

_____

PHOTO/DRAWING:

Location: _____

Date: _____ Weather: _____ Temperature: _____

Start time: _____ End time: _____ Total distance: _____

Hike rating: ☆ ☆ ☆ ☆ ☆ Difficulty: 1 2 3 4 5

Trail type: _____ Elevation gain/loss: _____

Trail(s): _____
_____

Terrain: _____
_____

Companions: _____
_____
_____

Facilities / Water availability?: _____
_____
_____

Observations (nature, wildlife, other): _____
_____
_____
_____

Favorite moment: _____
_____
_____

To do next time: _____
_____
_____

Notes:

_____

_____

_____

_____

_____

_____

_____

_____

_____

_____

Photo/Drawing:

Location: _____

Date: _____ Weather: _____ Temperature: _____

Start time: _____ End time: _____ Total distance: _____

Hike rating: ☆ ☆ ☆ ☆ ☆   Difficulty: 1 2 3 4 5

Trail type: _____ Elevation gain/loss: _____

Trail(s): _____
_____

Terrain: _____
_____

Companions: _____
_____
_____

Facilities / Water availability?: _____
_____
_____

Observations (nature, wildlife, other): _____
_____
_____

Favorite moment: _____
_____
_____

To do next time: _____
_____
_____

NOTES:

_____

_____

_____

_____

_____

_____

_____

_____

_____

_____

_____

PHOTO/DRAWING:

Location: _____

Date: _____ Weather: _____ Temperature: _____

Start time: _____ End time: _____ Total distance: _____

Hike rating: ☆ ☆ ☆ ☆ ☆   Difficulty: 1 2 3 4 5

Trail type: _____ Elevation gain/loss: _____

Trail(s): _____

_____

Terrain: _____

_____

Companions: _____

_____

_____

Facilities / Water availability?: _____

_____

_____

Observations (nature, wildlife, other): _____

_____

_____

Favorite moment: _____

_____

_____

To do next time: _____

_____

_____

NOTES:

_____

_____

_____

_____

_____

_____

_____

_____

_____

_____

PHOTO/DRAWING:

Location: _____

Date: _____ Weather: _____ Temperature: _____

Start time: _____ End time: _____ Total distance: _____

Hike rating: ☆ ☆ ☆ ☆ ☆   Difficulty: 1 2 3 4 5

Trail type: _____ Elevation gain/loss: _____

Trail(s): _____
_____

Terrain: _____
_____

Companions: _____
_____
_____

Facilities / Water availability?: _____
_____
_____

Observations (nature, wildlife, other): _____
_____
_____

Favorite moment: _____
_____
_____

To do next time: _____
_____
_____

NOTES:

_____

_____

_____

_____

_____

_____

_____

_____

_____

_____

_____

PHOTO/DRAWING:

Location: _____

Date: _____ Weather: _____ Temperature: _____

Start time: _____ End time: _____ Total distance: _____

Hike rating: ☆ ☆ ☆ ☆ ☆   Difficulty: 1 2 3 4 5

Trail type: _____ Elevation gain/loss: _____

Trail(s): _____

_____

Terrain: _____

_____

Companions: _____

_____

_____

Facilities / Water availability?: _____

_____

_____

Observations (nature, wildlife, other): _____

_____

_____

Favorite moment: _____

_____

_____

To do next time: _____

_____

_____

NOTES:

_____

_____

_____

_____

_____

_____

_____

_____

_____

_____

PHOTO/DRAWING:

Location: _____

Date: _____ Weather: _____ Temperature: _____

Start time: _____ End time: _____ Total distance: _____

Hike rating: ☆ ☆ ☆ ☆ ☆   Difficulty: 1 2 3 4 5

Trail type: _____ Elevation gain/loss: _____

Trail(s): _____

_____

Terrain: _____

_____

Companions: _____

_____

_____

Facilities / Water availability?: _____

_____

_____

Observations (nature, wildlife, other): _____

_____

_____

Favorite moment: _____

_____

_____

To do next time: _____

_____

_____

NOTES:

_____

_____

_____

_____

_____

_____

_____

_____

_____

_____

PHOTO/DRAWING:

LOCATION: _____

DATE: _____ WEATHER: _____ TEMPERATURE: _____

START TIME: _____ END TIME: _____ TOTAL DISTANCE: _____

HIKE RATING: ☆ ☆ ☆ ☆ ☆   DIFFICULTY: 1 2 3 4 5

TRAIL TYPE: _____ ELEVATION GAIN/LOSS: _____

TRAIL(S): _____

_____

TERRAIN: _____

_____

COMPANIONS: _____

_____

_____

FACILITIES / WATER AVAILABILITY?: _____

_____

_____

OBSERVATIONS (NATURE, WILDLIFE, OTHER): _____

_____

_____

FAVORITE MOMENT: _____

_____

_____

TO DO NEXT TIME: _____

_____

_____

NOTES:

_____

_____

_____

_____

_____

_____

_____

_____

_____

_____

PHOTO/DRAWING:

Location: _____

Date: _____ Weather: _____ Temperature: _____

Start time: _____ End time: _____ Total distance: _____

Hike rating: ☆ ☆ ☆ ☆ ☆   Difficulty: 1 2 3 4 5

Trail type: _____ Elevation gain/loss: _____

Trail(s): _____
_____

Terrain: _____
_____

Companions: _____
_____
_____

Facilities / Water availability?: _____
_____
_____

Observations (nature, wildlife, other): _____
_____
_____

Favorite moment: _____
_____
_____

To do next time: _____
_____
_____

NOTES:

_____

_____

_____

_____

_____

_____

_____

_____

_____

_____

PHOTO/DRAWING:

Location: _____

Date: _____ Weather: _____ Temperature: _____

Start time: _____ End time: _____ Total distance: _____

Hike rating: ☆ ☆ ☆ ☆ ☆ Difficulty: 1 2 3 4 5

Trail type: _____ Elevation gain/loss: _____

Trail(s): _____

_____

Terrain: _____

_____

Companions: _____

_____

_____

Facilities / Water availability?: _____

_____

_____

Observations (nature, wildlife, other): _____

_____

_____

Favorite moment: _____

_____

_____

To do next time: _____

_____

_____

NOTES:

_____

_____

_____

_____

_____

_____

_____

_____

_____

_____

PHOTO/DRAWING:

Location: _____

Date: _____ Weather: _____ Temperature: _____

Start time: _____ End time: _____ Total distance: _____

Hike rating: ☆ ☆ ☆ ☆ ☆   Difficulty: 1 2 3 4 5

Trail type: _____ Elevation gain/loss: _____

Trail(s): _____

_____

Terrain: _____

_____

Companions: _____

_____

_____

Facilities / Water availability?: _____

_____

_____

Observations (nature, wildlife, other): _____

_____

_____

Favorite moment: _____

_____

_____

To do next time: _____

_____

_____

Notes:

_____

_____

_____

_____

_____

_____

_____

_____

_____

_____

_____

Photo/Drawing:

Location: _____

Date: _____ Weather: _____ Temperature: _____

Start time: _____ End time: _____ Total distance: _____

Hike rating: ☆ ☆ ☆ ☆ ☆   Difficulty: 1 2 3 4 5

Trail type: _____ Elevation gain/loss: _____

Trail(s): _____
_____

Terrain: _____
_____

Companions: _____
_____
_____

Facilities / Water availability?: _____
_____
_____

Observations (nature, wildlife, other): _____
_____
_____

Favorite moment: _____
_____
_____

To do next time: _____
_____
_____

NOTES:

_____

_____

_____

_____

_____

_____

_____

_____

_____

_____

PHOTO/DRAWING:

Location: _____

Date: _____ Weather: _____ Temperature: _____

Start time: _____ End time: _____ Total distance: _____

Hike rating: ☆ ☆ ☆ ☆ ☆   Difficulty: 1 2 3 4 5

Trail type: _____ Elevation gain/loss: _____

Trail(s): _____
_____

Terrain: _____
_____

Companions: _____
_____
_____

Facilities / Water availability?: _____
_____
_____

Observations (nature, wildlife, other): _____
_____
_____

Favorite moment: _____
_____
_____

To do next time: _____
_____
_____

NOTES:

_____

_____

_____

_____

_____

_____

_____

_____

_____

_____

PHOTO/DRAWING:

Location: _____

Date: _____ Weather: _____ Temperature: _____

Start time: _____ End time: _____ Total distance: _____

Hike rating: ☆ ☆ ☆ ☆ ☆   Difficulty: 1 2 3 4 5

Trail type: _____ Elevation gain/loss: _____

Trail(s): _____

_____

Terrain: _____

_____

Companions: _____

_____

_____

Facilities / Water availability?: _____

_____

_____

Observations (nature, wildlife, other): _____

_____

_____

Favorite moment: _____

_____

_____

To do next time: _____

_____

_____

NOTES:

_____

_____

_____

_____

_____

_____

_____

_____

_____

_____

_____

PHOTO/DRAWING:

Location: _____

Date: _____ Weather: _____ Temperature: _____

Start time: _____ End time: _____ Total distance: _____

Hike rating: ☆ ☆ ☆ ☆ ☆   Difficulty: 1 2 3 4 5

Trail type: _____ Elevation gain/loss: _____

Trail(s): _____

_____

Terrain: _____

_____

Companions: _____

_____

_____

Facilities / Water availability?: _____

_____

_____

Observations (nature, wildlife, other): _____

_____

_____

Favorite moment: _____

_____

_____

To do next time: _____

_____

_____

NOTES:

_____
_____
_____
_____
_____
_____
_____
_____
_____
_____

PHOTO/DRAWING:

Location: _____

Date: _____ Weather: _____ Temperature: _____

Start time: _____ End time: _____ Total distance: _____

Hike rating: ☆ ☆ ☆ ☆ ☆   Difficulty: 1 2 3 4 5

Trail type: _____ Elevation gain/loss: _____

Trail(s): _____

_____

Terrain: _____

_____

Companions: _____

_____

_____

Facilities / Water availability?: _____

_____

_____

Observations (nature, wildlife, other): _____

_____

_____

Favorite moment: _____

_____

_____

To do next time: _____

_____

_____

NOTES:

_____

_____

_____

_____

_____

_____

_____

_____

_____

_____

PHOTO/DRAWING:

Location: _____

Date: _____ Weather: _____ Temperature: _____

Start time: _____ End time: _____ Total distance: _____

Hike rating: ☆ ☆ ☆ ☆ ☆   Difficulty: 1 2 3 4 5

Trail type: _____ Elevation gain/loss: _____

Trail(s): _____

_____

Terrain: _____

_____

Companions: _____

_____

_____

Facilities / Water availability?: _____

_____

_____

Observations (nature, wildlife, other): _____

_____

_____

Favorite moment: _____

_____

_____

To do next time: _____

_____

_____

NOTES:

_____

_____

_____

_____

_____

_____

_____

_____

_____

_____

_____

PHOTO/DRAWING:

Location: _____

Date: _____ Weather: _____ Temperature: _____

Start time: _____ End time: _____ Total distance: _____

Hike rating: ☆ ☆ ☆ ☆ ☆   Difficulty: 1 2 3 4 5

Trail type: _____ Elevation gain/loss: _____

Trail(s): _____
_____

Terrain: _____
_____

Companions: _____
_____
_____

Facilities / Water availability?: _____
_____
_____

Observations (nature, wildlife, other): _____
_____
_____

Favorite moment: _____
_____
_____

To do next time: _____
_____
_____

NOTES: _____

_____

_____

_____

_____

_____

_____

_____

_____

_____

_____

PHOTO/DRAWING:

Location: _____

Date: _____ Weather: _____ Temperature: _____

Start time: _____ End time: _____ Total distance: _____

Hike rating: ☆ ☆ ☆ ☆ ☆   Difficulty: 1 2 3 4 5

Trail type: _____ Elevation gain/loss: _____

Trail(s): _____

_____

Terrain: _____

_____

Companions: _____

_____

_____

Facilities / Water availability?: _____

_____

_____

Observations (nature, wildlife, other): _____

_____

_____

Favorite moment: _____

_____

_____

To do next time: _____

_____

_____

NOTES:

_____

_____

_____

_____

_____

_____

_____

_____

_____

_____

PHOTO/DRAWING:

Location: _____

Date: _____ Weather: _____ Temperature: _____

Start time: _____ End time: _____ Total distance: _____

Hike rating: ☆ ☆ ☆ ☆ ☆   Difficulty: 1 2 3 4 5

Trail type: _____ Elevation gain/loss: _____

Trail(s): _____
_____

Terrain: _____
_____

Companions: _____
_____
_____

Facilities / Water availability?: _____
_____
_____

Observations (nature, wildlife, other): _____
_____
_____

Favorite moment: _____
_____
_____

To do next time: _____
_____
_____

NOTES:

_____
_____
_____
_____
_____
_____
_____
_____
_____

PHOTO/DRAWING:

Location: _____

Date: _____ Weather: _____ Temperature: _____

Start time: _____ End time: _____ Total distance: _____

Hike rating: ☆ ☆ ☆ ☆ ☆   Difficulty: 1 2 3 4 5

Trail type: _____ Elevation gain/loss: _____

Trail(s): _____

_____

Terrain: _____

_____

Companions: _____

_____

_____

Facilities / Water availability?: _____

_____

_____

Observations (nature, wildlife, other): _____

_____

_____

Favorite moment: _____

_____

_____

To do next time: _____

_____

_____

NOTES:

_____

_____

_____

_____

_____

_____

_____

_____

_____

_____

_____

PHOTO/DRAWING:

LOCATION: _____

DATE: _____ WEATHER: _____ TEMPERATURE: _____

START TIME: _____ END TIME: _____ TOTAL DISTANCE: _____

HIKE RATING: ☆ ☆ ☆ ☆ ☆   DIFFICULTY: 1 2 3 4 5

TRAIL TYPE: _____ ELEVATION GAIN/LOSS: _____

TRAIL(S): _____

_____

TERRAIN: _____

_____

COMPANIONS: _____

_____

_____

FACILITIES / WATER AVAILABILITY?: _____

_____

_____

OBSERVATIONS (NATURE, WILDLIFE, OTHER): _____

_____

_____

FAVORITE MOMENT: _____

_____

_____

TO DO NEXT TIME: _____

_____

_____

NOTES: _____

_____

_____

_____

_____

_____

_____

_____

_____

_____

PHOTO/DRAWING:

Location: _____

Date: _____ Weather: _____ Temperature: _____

Start time: _____ End time: _____ Total distance: _____

Hike rating: ☆ ☆ ☆ ☆ ☆   Difficulty: 1 2 3 4 5

Trail type: _____ Elevation gain/loss: _____

Trail(s): _____

_____

Terrain: _____

_____

Companions: _____

_____

_____

Facilities / Water availability?: _____

_____

_____

Observations (nature, wildlife, other): _____

_____

_____

Favorite moment: _____

_____

_____

To do next time: _____

_____

_____

NOTES: _____

_____

_____

_____

_____

_____

_____

_____

_____

_____

PHOTO/DRAWING:

Location: _____

Date: _____ Weather: _____ Temperature: _____

Start time: _____ End time: _____ Total distance: _____

Hike rating: ☆ ☆ ☆ ☆ ☆   Difficulty: 1 2 3 4 5

Trail type: _____ Elevation gain/loss: _____

Trail(s): _____
_____

Terrain: _____
_____

Companions: _____
_____
_____

Facilities / Water availability?: _____
_____
_____

Observations (nature, wildlife, other): _____
_____
_____

Favorite moment: _____
_____
_____

To do next time: _____
_____
_____

NOTES:

_____

_____

_____

_____

_____

_____

_____

_____

_____

_____

PHOTO/DRAWING:

Location: _____

Date: _____ Weather: _____ Temperature: _____

Start time: _____ End time: _____ Total distance: _____

Hike rating: ☆ ☆ ☆ ☆ ☆   Difficulty: 1 2 3 4 5

Trail type: _____ Elevation gain/loss: _____

Trail(s): _____

_____

Terrain: _____

_____

Companions: _____

_____

_____

Facilities / Water availability?: _____

_____

_____

Observations (nature, wildlife, other): _____

_____

_____

Favorite moment: _____

_____

_____

To do next time: _____

_____

_____

NOTES: _____

_____

_____

_____

_____

_____

_____

_____

_____

_____

PHOTO/DRAWING:

LOCATION: _____

DATE: _____ WEATHER: _____ TEMPERATURE: _____

START TIME: _____ END TIME: _____ TOTAL DISTANCE: _____

HIKE RATING: ☆ ☆ ☆ ☆ ☆   DIFFICULTY: 1 2 3 4 5

TRAIL TYPE: _____ ELEVATION GAIN/LOSS: _____

TRAIL(S): _____
_____

TERRAIN: _____
_____

COMPANIONS: _____
_____
_____

FACILITIES / WATER AVAILABILITY?: _____
_____
_____

OBSERVATIONS (NATURE, WILDLIFE, OTHER): _____
_____
_____

FAVORITE MOMENT: _____
_____
_____

TO DO NEXT TIME: _____
_____
_____

NOTES:

_____

_____

_____

_____

_____

_____

_____

_____

_____

_____

_____

_____

PHOTO/DRAWING:

Location: _____

Date: _____ Weather: _____ Temperature: _____

Start time: _____ End time: _____ Total distance: _____

Hike rating: ☆ ☆ ☆ ☆ ☆   Difficulty: 1 2 3 4 5

Trail type: _____ Elevation gain/loss: _____

Trail(s): _____

_____

Terrain: _____

_____

Companions: _____

_____

_____

Facilities / Water availability?: _____

_____

_____

Observations (nature, wildlife, other): _____

_____

_____

Favorite moment: _____

_____

_____

To do next time: _____

_____

_____

NOTES:

_____

_____

_____

_____

_____

_____

_____

_____

_____

_____

PHOTO/DRAWING:

Location: _____

Date: _____ Weather: _____ Temperature: _____

Start time: _____ End time: _____ Total distance: _____

Hike rating: ☆ ☆ ☆ ☆ ☆   Difficulty: 1 2 3 4 5

Trail type: _____ Elevation gain/loss: _____

Trail(s): _____

_____

Terrain: _____

_____

Companions: _____

_____

_____

Facilities / Water availability?: _____

_____

_____

Observations (nature, wildlife, other): _____

_____

_____

Favorite moment: _____

_____

_____

To do next time: _____

_____

_____

NOTES:

_____

_____

_____

_____

_____

_____

_____

_____

_____

_____

PHOTO/DRAWING: